Best in Snow

April Pulley Sayre

Beach Lane Books   New York   London   Toronto   Sydney   New Delhi

A freeze.

A breeze.

A cloud.

It snows.

Snowflakes land
on a squirrel's nose.

Snow sails.

It settles,

shows shapes,

dusts wings.

Snowfall quickens

and thickens.

Snow clumps and clings.

But then . . .

Wind sifts.

Snow drifts.

Sun shines.

Water seeps.

Crystals feather

as ice creeps.

Air warms.

Snow softens.

It drip,

drip,

drips.

Snowmelt
forms
icicle
tips.

Down below,
soil mixes with snow.

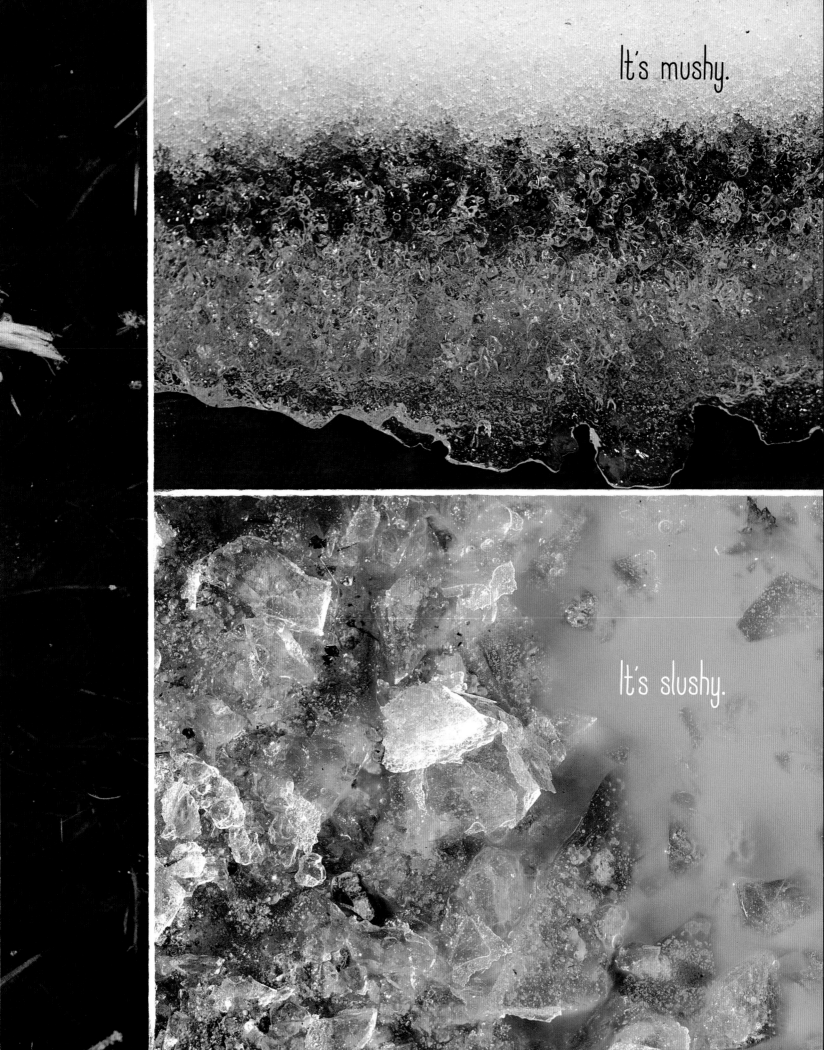

It's mushy.

It's slushy.

Until . . .

Another freeze.

Another b r e e z e.

Another cloud.

It snows.

And another snowflake lands . . .

on a squirrel's nose.

Secrets of Snow

Snow has a long journey before it reaches a squirrel—or you. Most of the moisture that becomes snow evaporates from lakes, rivers, the ocean, or other bodies of water. Another source is water that evaporates from plant leaves and the ground. A tiny fraction also comes from water vapor that forms directly from snow without first turning into liquid. All this moisture rises to become part of a cloud. A snowstorm is on its way.

A freeze. A breeze. A cloud.

Pushed by winds, clouds travel, carrying moisture to new areas. Inside clouds, water vapor becomes liquid as it condenses onto a nucleus of dust or ice. It's so cold inside clouds, the liquid water freezes. Once an ice particle is formed, more ice particles condense onto the first one, forming snowflake arms. Snowflake arms may grow within the cloud, or as the snowflake falls.

Snow sails.

Sometimes snow falls in tiny single flakes, and sometimes it falls in big clumps of many flakes. Sometimes it is light and fluffy; at other times it is heavy and compacted. Air temperature and humidity affect the size and texture of the flakes.

Snow shows shapes.

Wind often pushes flakes so they fall at an angle rather than straight down. They may plaster one side of a tree branch but leave the other side bare. The contrast between the dark, bare areas and the bright snow outlines trees and other outdoor features. The landscape can look like an ink drawing. Snow, by covering up some things, helps us see shapes that were there all along.

Snow clumps and clings.

As snow ages, it changes. Melting and refreezing can form an icy crust atop the snow. Small, lightweight animals may walk on the ice crust without their feet falling into the soft snow beneath.

Wind sifts. Snow drifts.

On extremely cold, sunny days, new snow may sparkle as it falls. Snow sparkle is light that bounces off the flat faces of snow and ice crystals. Older fallen snow constantly changes. Wind scours the snow's surface. It lifts fine snow particles, sorts them, and moves them to new places. Wind-driven snow may pile up, forming drifts.

Crystals feather.
Warm days. Cold nights. Freeze and thaw. Shifts in temperature change the icy, snowy landscape. A snowbank melts and refreezes, creating ice that cracks along jagged lines. Snowmelt seeping out of a soggy log or plant stem refreezes into elaborate feather shapes. Water vapor in the air deposits on a window, creating frost. That frost melts, and drips begin to form, but the drips refreeze into round shapes before they can slide off the glass.

Snowmelt forms icicle tips.
Melted snow drips off houses, hillsides, and other elevated structures. If the air temperature is cold enough, these drips refreeze to form icicles.

It's mushy. It's slushy.
Slush is made of liquid water and granules of ice. Often there is mud mixed in. When cold temperatures return, slush can freeze, making streets and sidewalks slippery.

Bodies of Water

Many people depend on snow for drinking water, yet never even see snow. This snowfall happens far away, up in mountains. In spring, the snow melts and flows into rivers and down into valleys that would otherwise be dry. The water is then pumped into towns and cities and flows out of faucets in places such as Los Angeles.

Often people call lakes, rivers, streams, and the ocean "bodies of water." But you have a body, and it's made mostly of water too! About two-thirds of the human body is water. That water has been rain. It has been snow. It has been ocean water, lake water, stream water, and cloud water. As to whether the water in your body once fell as a snowflake onto a squirrel's nose, well . . . it's possible!

To dig into more snow, consult these books:

Cassino, Mark, with Jon Nelson, Ph.D. *The Story of Snow.* San Francisco: Chronicle Books, 2009.

Libbrecht, Kenneth. *The Secret Life of a Snowflake: An Up-Close Look at the Art and Science of Snowflakes.* Minneapolis, MN: Voyageur Press, 2010. A taste of Libbrecht's photos and explanations of snow and frost formations are on his site, snowcrystals.com.

Martin, Jacqueline Briggs. *Snowflake Bentley.* Boston: Houghton Mifflin, 1998.

Messner, Kate. *Over and Under the Snow.* San Francisco: Chronicle Books, 2014.

Sidman, Joyce. *Winter Bees & Other Poems of the Cold.* Boston: HMH Books for Young Readers, 2014.

JP
SAY

16-11-29
Bot 17⁹⁹/13⁵⁷

For the Pulley Ski Team:
Skiers to the traces! Everybody in their places!

THANK YOU. Andrea Welch, for putting heart and imagination into this work. Thank you,
Lauren "Raindrops" Rille, for playing in snow and lending it some of your sparkle.
For scientific review, I appreciate the assistance of climatologist Dr. Steven Quiring,
associate professor, Texas A&M; Dr. Kenneth G. Libbrecht, Professor of Physics,
Caltech; Sam Lashley, senior meteorologist, National Weather Service, Northern
Indiana Office; and Mike Hoffman, chief meteorologist for WNDU-TV and Ag Day/
US Farm Report meteorologist. Thank you also to the staff of St. Joseph County Parks.
Part of this book was photographed at St. Patrick's County Park.

BEACH LANE BOOKS An imprint of Simon & Schuster Children's Publishing Division • 1230 Avenue of the Americas, New York, New York 10020 • Copyright ©
2016 by April Pulley Sayre • All rights reserved, including the right of reproduction in whole or in part in any form. • BEACH LANE BOOKS is a trademark of Simon & Schuster,
Inc. • For information about special discounts for bulk purchases, please contact Simon & Schuster Special Sales at 1-866-506-1949 or business@simonandschuster.com.
• The Simon & Schuster Speakers Bureau can bring authors to your live event. For more information or to book an event, contact the Simon & Schuster Speakers Bureau at
1-866-248-3049 or visit our website at www.simonspeakers.com. • Book design by Lauren Rille • The text for this book is set in Quickrest and Bodoni. • Manufactured in
China • 0716 SCP • First Edition • 10 9 8 7 6 5 4 3 2 1 • CIP data for this book is available from the Library of Congress. • ISBN 978-1-4814-5916-7 (hardcover)
• ISBN 978-1-4814-5917-4 (eBook)